How the Chinese Teach English

by
Rhea A. Ashmore
and
Chu Xianhua

ISBN 0-87367-894-X

Bloomington, Indiana

Table of Contents

Introduction

Worldwide, approximately 1.1 billion non-native speakers are developing their English language skills for study, work, travel, and personal enjoyment (Graddol 1997). China is the world's largest market for language-study programs, with approximately 165 million children and adults studying English (Lingo Media 2002). Modernization and China's economic and social development have spurred nationwide English language fever. This fastback examines the teaching of English in the People's Republic of China and why it is such a prized literacy.

During spring 2001 Beijing Mayor Liu Qi announced that should the Olympics come to town, he would issue a directive calling for all cab drivers to learn English. Now that Beijing is the site for the 2008 Olympics, the goal is to have 100,000 "comfortable English speaking" citizens volunteer to serve at the Olympic Games. Furthermore, English is the required second language for the city's taxi drivers, tourist guides, government officials, and organizers and coordinators of the upcoming international sporting event ("Olympic Bidding Success" 2001).

The enthusiasm for learning English is contagious. Favorable events, such as China's entry to the World Trade Organization and the successful bid for the Olympics, have created a nationwide zeal for learning English. In October 2002 the Beijing Foreign Languages Festival highlighting English drew more than 50,000, including English-language professors, primary school students, taxi drivers, and policemen. The participants talked, sang songs, and watched movies in English. Primary school children are involved in a campaign called "I Teach Dad and Mom English." Language schools and English programs on television and radio are booming. Hundreds of schools are marketing English training courses, among them the New Oriental School. This business, founded in 1993, offers a variety of English courses, including training for the Test of English as a Foreign Language (TOEFL) and the Graduate Record Examination (GRE). Each year more than 150,000 students enroll in courses that run from 12 days to three months.

Web surveys demonstrate that salaries positively correlate with English proficiency. Those earning an average yearly income of more than 53,400 yuan (US$6,450) have a good command of English, while those with an average yearly income of approximately 31,200 yuan (US$3,770) maintain an intermediate level of English or lower ("Zeal to Learn Languages" 2002).

These national developments are having an effect on education in general. The Ministry of Education (MOE) recently directed schools to raise the quality of education by reforming the curriculum, textbooks, teaching methods, and assessment procedures. Strategies include purchasing international teaching materials, hiring foreign experts, and requiring key colleges and universities to instruct science, economics, and management courses in both Chinese and English. The MOE has mandated English as a compulsory subject for millions of primary school students.

Political and Educational Foundations

The world's third largest country in area, the People's Republic of China (PRC) is divided into 23 provinces, five autonomous regions, two special administrative regions, and four municipalities directly under the central government. Adopted on 4 December 1982, the *Constitution of the PRC* states, "The basic task of the nation in the years to come is to concentrate its effort on socialist modernization." In order to do so, "state organs" run the Chinese government: the National People's Congress (NPC), the highest division of state power, with its permanent body called the Standing Committee of the NPC; the President; the State Council; the Central Military Commission; the Supreme People's Court; and the Supreme People's Procuratorate.

Responsible for the daily running of the country, the State Council implements the principles and policies of the Communist Party of China, as well as the regulations and laws adopted by the NPC. The council is composed of a premier, vice-premiers, state councilors, ministers in charge of ministries and commissions, the auditorgeneral, and the secretary-general. Ministries include foreign affairs, national defense, science and technology, public safety, state security, justice, finance, and education. The Ministry of Education (MOE) is the supreme administrative authority for education. This unit coordinates educational undertakings, directs education reform, and formulates education policies.

Education Policies

On 12 April 1986 the Fourth Plenary Session of the Sixth People's Congress approved the Law on Compulsory Education. This law provides all children at least nine years of formal schooling, six years of primary education and three years of junior secondary education. A rigid and comprehensive examination system determines whether a student attends senior secondary schools. Prior to 2001, the primary school curriculum included moral education, Chinese, mathematics, natural science, geography, history, physical education, music, fine arts, and physical labor. Only primary schools in cities and some in central towns at the county level informally offered English for fifth- and sixth-graders (Ashmore and Cao 1997).

The curriculum changed when, on 18 January 2001, the MOE issued *A Guidance for Energetic Implementation of English in Primary Schools* (Ministry of Education 2001*a*) and in June 2001 issued the *Outline of Curriculum Reform in Basic Education (Experimental Version)* (Ministry of Education 2001*c*) (see Appendices A and B for complete translations). The State Council enforced these documents by declaring that, in order to further reform and accelerate "quality education," English would gradually be offered in primary schools on the district level.

The English mandates affect 582,291 primary schools, 5,861,000 full-time primary school teachers, and 135,480,000 primary school students (Department of Planning and Construction 1999). The goals are to activate children's interest in learning English and to promote their communicative skills. English is to be offered four times per week; teaching methods should include innovative teaching models, methods, and materials, including textbooks, multimedia, television, tapes, and CDs.

The rationale for English is clear. China's reform movement, characterized by enhanced exchanges with other countries, international economic trade, and tourism, has affected social life. Reform, coupled with swift developments in science and technology and economic globalization, demands English mastery. Since the 1980s, primary school English education has expanded; and millions of primary students are learning English. Therefore, in order to implement the decisions by the Communist Party of China's fifth plenary meeting of the 15th committee and the Third National Congress on Education and to promote the strategic guiding philosophy that education is key to modernization and the future, the MOE listed English in the primary schools as a priority in the reform of basic curriculum.

Mandates are easier passed than enacted. Except for four municipalities — Beijing, Shanghai, Tianjin, and

Chongqing — the status of implementing English in the primary schools in the provinces and autonomous regions on Mainland China is not satisfactory. For example, by the end of year 2000, seven counties in Tibet did not offer English courses in the middle schools. Significant problems include dated instructional methods and lack of systematic course books for primary and middle schools. Liu (2001) states that high school students receive more than 800 teaching hours in six years of learning English; however, most of them are still "deaf and dumb" in English, with barely 2,000 words learned.

The biggest hindrance is the severe shortage of qualified English teachers. There is only one English teacher per 10 schools, and most teachers are practicing in urban schools. In western, rural, and remote regions, English teachers are scarce. Most teachers were educated in the late 1970s, and the majority of the 500,000 secondary English teachers and 200,000 primary school English teachers are not qualified. According to the Teacher Personnel Department of the MOE (2001), only 13% of primary school teachers earned diplomas from junior colleges or above.

Teacher Training

Teachers in China are trained according to the level at which they plan to teach. Teachers for nursery schools, kindergartens, and primary schools are prepared at the secondary level. Secondary school teachers and those who will teach in higher education are prepared at the higher education level.

At the secondary education level, specialized secondary schools, or normal schools, enroll junior secondary school graduates for three to four years of additional schooling. General normal schools train teachers for primary (elementary) schools and provide advanced courses for inservice training. Table 1 presents the required coursework for primary English teachers.

The State Council's document, "Reform and Development of Basic Education" (2001) cites the need to perfect the teacher training system and to reform the personnel system. Cultivating a cadre of highly qualified teachers is key to promoting high-quality education and English teaching. In order to reinforce these needs, the MOE issued the following:

> 1. Under the guidance of the local education authority, normal colleges at different levels should offer training programs to both leading teachers and assistant teachers in the forms of part-time workshops and summer intensive training sessions. In this manner both groups of teachers can achieve the requirements for primary school teaching.
>
> 2. To raise the capacity and capability of training primary school English teachers, normal schools and institutes should emphasize the development of the English education program.
>
> 3. Secondary normal schools should make English a required course, rather than an elective course.
>
> 4. Continue to run secondary foreign language schools; those normal schools with sufficient resources can be converted into secondary foreign language normal schools. Normal schools should be encouraged to offer specialized English programs. (State Council 2001)

Table 1. Required coursework for primary English teacher training.

		Semester					
		1	2	3	4		
		18wks	16wks	17wks	10wks		
	Basic courses	Hours/week				Total hrs	Credits
1	Marxist philosophy	2	2			68	4
2	Deng Xiaoping theory			2	2	54	4
3	Chinese language & literature	2	2	2	2	122	8
4	Advanced mathematics	2	2			68	4
5	Intro modern science	2				36	2
6	Computer principles/app	2	2	2	2	120	8
7	Physical education	2	2	2	2	120	8
	Subject-matter courses						
1	Integrated English	6	6	4	4	160	20
2	Audio-visual & oral practice	2	2	2	2	122	8
3	Short story reading	2	2			68	4
4	Grammar		2			32	2
5	Translation			2	2	54	4
6	Writing			2	2	54	3
7	Phonetics	2				36	2
	Educational courses						
1	Elementary ed: reform & development			2	2	54	2
2	Introduction to research in elementary education		2			32	2
3	Didactics			2	2	54	4
4	Instructional psychology	2	2			68	4
5	Calligraphy	1	1			34	2
6	Primary language art methodology	2	2			68	4
7	Primary mathematics methodology			2		34	2
8	Primary English methodology		2	2		66	
9	Fine arts	2	2	2	2	122	8
10	Youth activities	4	4	4	4	244	16
11	Student teaching				6 wks		
	Totals	35	37	32	28	1890	125

From School of Elementary Education, Hangzhou Teachers College, September, 2002.

Alternative certification routes for non-English major, inservice teachers are in the offing. On 16 September 2002, the Zhejiang Provincial Education Office issued *A Probative Certification Regulation for Inservice Primary School English Teachers.* According to the regulation, all teachers who have not majored in English education but are teaching English at primary schools must enroll in various required courses. Table 2 presents the one-year intensive training offered through the College of Education, Zhejiang University.

Table 2. One-year intensive training program for primary English teachers who did not major in English education.

	Coursework	Semester 1 18 wks	Semester 2 18 wks	Total instructional hours
1	Integrated English	9	9	324
2	Listening practice	4	4	144
3	Oral English	2	2	72
4	Grammar	3		54
5	Phonetics	2		36
6	Reading and writing		2	36
7	Methodology	2	3	90
	Total instructional hours	22	20	756
	Non-English class activities	3	3	108

From College of Education, Zhejiang University, 2001-2002 academic year.

Certification also requires passing the unified language proficiency and teaching ability tests, which are offered twice a year by the Provincial Examination Department. Teachers who fail to be certified by September 2005 will no longer be permitted to teach. The tests include: English language proficiency (the minimal requirement is the second level of the Public English Test System, PETS-2, which is equivalent to oral language proficiency at the senior high school graduate level); and language teaching ability as demonstrated by competence in primary school English teaching techniques.

National English proficiency is the barometer of China's standard of internationalization. The Chinese are actively promoting English education with sensitivity to transforming examination-oriented education into high-quality education, emphasizing ESP (English for Special Purposes) courses, enhancing interactive instruction, reinforcing international collaboration, using modern technology, and designing new textbooks.

Materials for Learning English

The year 2002 witnessed energetic efforts in implementing English courses in primary schools throughout China, especially in the large and medium-size cities. More courses mean more teaching materials. As the MOE advocates new teaching materials to create positive conditions for learning and teaching, many course books for English instruction are coming off the presses. Most textbooks are co-published by Chinese and foreign publishing companies. Prevalent English course books are *PEP Primary English* (2001), *New Standard English* (Ellis 2000), and *Cambridge Young Learners English* (Qiu, Wang, and Liang 2000). All of these programs focus on English as a communicative skill; lesson activities include listening, singing or chanting, saying, and doing.

PEP Primary English

People's Education Press (PEP), a subsidiary of the MOE and the State Publication Administration, publishes about 80% of the K-12 education materials for all subjects throughout China. With a readership of more than 150 million students, PEP has the mandate to publish and distribute materials to meet the requirements of the new curriculum developed by the MOE.

Lingo Media, a Canadian publishing service, has four programs in development with PEP. Three series target the elementary English market: *PEP Primary English* (PPE) for grades 3-6, *Starting Line* for grades 1-6, and *Beginning English for Young Learners* for grades 1 and 2. The *Junior Reading Comprehension* series is intended for junior middle school students, or grades seven to nine.

The PPE series consists of eight student books (two per grade), 16 audiocassettes, and four teacher resource books. Supplementary materials are now in production. The 7" x 10" student book's contents are arranged in "units" and "recycles," or reviews. Following are the contents in student book 1:

Unit 1: Hello
Unit 2: Look at Me
Unit 3: Let's Paint
Recycle 1
Unit 4: We Love Animals
Unit 5: Let's Eat
Unit 6: Happy Birthday
Recycle 2
Words in Each Unit
Vocabulary

The units contain colorful cartoons of people and animals talking, plus activities labeled A, B, and C. Activities in section A are "Let's Talk," which promotes dialogues; "Let's Play," which encourages actions and dialogues; "Let's Learn," with picture and word identification; "Let's Do," in which written statements dictate actions; "Let's Make," in which the reader makes something; and "Let's Sing," which provides lyrics and music. Activities in section B are similar to those in section A (Let's Talk, Let's Play, Let's Learn, Let's Do) with the addition of "Let's Check," in which the reader selects the correct picture based on verbal cues, and "Let's Chant," in which the reader recites phrases. Contents in section C are "Story Time," comics-style readings; "Culture," which infuses geography, and "Let's Sing," which concludes the lesson with another song.

The "Recycle" sections review vocabulary and include assessment based on oral reading, listening, and doing: Listen and number, listen and draw, listen and match, listen and color, and listen and choose. At the end of the student book, specialized vocabulary is listed by unit and also alphabetically.

New Standard English

Published in 2000 by Foreign Language Teaching and Research Press and Macmillan, *New Standard English* (NSE) includes textbooks ranging from grade 1 or grade 3 in primary school, depending on when English is introduced, to senior 3 in middle school, or grade 9. In 18 of the 23 provinces, many experimental primary schools have adopted this series, bringing sales of more than 2 million sets of textbooks (FLTRP 2002).

The textbooks consist of a student book, an activity book, and a teacher book. There is one set for each semester. For example, as most schools teach English starting in grade 3, the texts are labeled 3A for fall semester and 3B for spring semester. The 8" x 11" softbound student book's contents are termed "modules," and each module contains "units." Each unit contains similar yet varied sections. For example, the sections in 3A, Module 12 Food, are: listen and point, listen and repeat, act it out, listen and say, ask and answer, chant, sing, and ask and answer and then say. The number of modules ranges from 10 to 12 per text.

Similar to PPE, these modules contain colorful cartoons of people and animals talking; and each module is arranged in three units. Activities in unit 1 are comics-formatted dialogues and listening and acting activities. Activities in unit 2 include more listening and doing or saying activities. Activities in unit 3 further promote listening and saying, singing, or playing games. The final review module also contains three units and provides an overall review. At the end of the student book, a word list alphabetically presents all of the words introduced in the book.

Cambridge Young Learners English

As more Chinese parents realize the importance of English, they are sending their children to learning centers outside school to study English. Growing in popularity, the Cambridge Young Learners English (CYLE) is one of these programs. Compared to the English courses offered by most public schools, this program offers several advantages: smaller class size, certified teachers, variation in teaching methods, and more choices for children of different ages. Parents pay for their children's learning, and students take tests to demonstrate their language competency.

CYLE is officially supervised and accompanied by a nationwide CYLE test held twice a year that assesses the English proficiency of primary learners. Program tuition is 500 to 800 yuan ($60 to $100) per year and includes 120 to 150 hours of instruction. More than 4 million children have participated in the program, and 20,000 teachers have been certified (CYLE 2001). In Zhejiang Province there are 116 registered CYLE learning centers with approximately 35,800 young learners, and the number is growing steadily.

In December 2000 the Sino-British Center compiled a series of course books related to the CYLE tests. Manufactured by Beijing Xinzhitang Education and Network Technologies and published by Xi'an Traffic University Press, *Cambridge Young Learners English* (*CYLE*) are the texts used to teach English and prepare candidates for the tests (Qiu, Wang, and Liang 2000). Designed for children ages six to 12, the series is based on the common CYLE tests syllabi and the English Teaching Syllabus compiled by the MOE for nine-year compulsory education. The publishers claim that the content and format reflect children's cognitive abilities and psychological traits. Features of the series include:

- Standard language conventions, including vocabulary, grammar, and pronunciation.
- Content reflecting Asian children's life, including dialogues, exercises, songs, and games.
- Colorful pictures illustrating the written materials.

- Listening, speaking, reading, spelling, and writing integrated with the teaching materials.
- A teachers' manual and a parents' book.
- Instructional activities presented in units paralleling the schedule of primary and junior middle schools.

Four levels are available: Pre-starters, Starters, Movers, and Flyers. A complete set of teaching materials (two books, four tapes, and a DVD explaining the scheme and the tests) accompanies each level. Supplementary materials — tapes, manuals, wall maps, and word cards — also are offered.

There are 18 units per text. Each unit contains similar but varied sections. The sections in "Starters, Unit 1: What's Your Name?" are "Let's Talk About It," "Let's Read," "Let's Practice," "Let's Sing," and exercises, including fill in the missing word, act it, let's chant, and answer the question in writing. The sections in "Starters, Unit 16: What's for Breakfast?" are "Let's Talk," "Match and Answer," "Let's Play," "Read and Act," "Read and Write," and exercises, including word find, listen and write, let's chant, listen and draw, and write your own menu.

Following the format of the above English texts, the 8½" x 11" softbound book uses colorful cartoons of people and animals interacting. Activities in Unit 1 involve talking, reading, practicing, and singing accompanied with exercises that require reading, acting, chanting, and writing. The final review unit contains activities that involve reading and writing, reading and identifying, asking and answering, listening and identifying, making guesses, coloring, and listening and reading a final story. At the conclusion of the book is an alphabetized comprehensive word list, including parts of speech, a name list, and removable stickers.

Evaluating the Programs

After examining several approaches to program evaluation, including *Features of Literacy Programs: A Decision-Making Matrix* (NCTE 2002), *Building a Knowledge Base in Reading* (Braunger and Lewis 1997), and the Center for the Improvement of Early Reading Achievement's 2001 guidelines for teaching children to read, we developed a rubric that was suitable for assessing *PPE*, *NSE*, and *CYLE*. We chose eight criteria: intended audience, media / tools, participant structure, instructional approaches, comprehension, word recognition, reading / writing connections, and assessment. Each criterion had several features. For example, the intended audience criterion included primary, elementary, middle school, or high school. Based on the eight criteria, we evaluated the contents of the three English textbooks.

In summary, the English textbooks are strong in the use of scripted texts, audiotapes, software, whole-class instruction, skills instruction, drill and practice, and vocabulary. On the other hand, the texts are lacking in the use of children's literature, video, small and ad hoc grouping, student-generated topics, phonemic awareness, and writing.

English Teaching in Action

Let's observe a public, primary classroom in which English is being taught. The 50 students, usually wearing uniforms, are seated in rows with two children per double desk. Using predominately whole-group instruction, the teachers engage their students in listening, reciting, and chanting activities in English. The students are well disciplined and either recite in unison or eagerly raise their hands to be recognized. Most lessons include cassette players and audiotapes and overhead projections that supplement the written materials. The textbooks, including the teacher's manual, student book, and student activity book, guide the instruction.

In addition to public schools, the number of experimental and private schools in China is increasing. These schools feature smaller classes, more instruction per week, and innovative instruction. In general, where public schools usually do not start teaching English until third grade, the experimental and private schools begin teaching English in the first grade. The experimental and private schools have more English classes each week than do the public schools, and they use a variety of instructional techniques that are not often used in the public schools.

English lessons in the public schools are structured and uniform. The *PEP English Teacher's Manual Book 1* (2001), which is based on the MOE's 2001 *Basic Requirements for Primary English Teaching (Experimental Version)* (see Appendix C for a complete translation), offers the following English lesson design:

1. Warm-up / Revision
   Sing an English song learned in a previous lesson; students act while singing.
   Teacher and students (standing up) exchange greetings.
   Review English words by listening and recitation.
2. Presentation
   Demonstration: The teacher takes out an empty bag and says the words, *pen, ruler, eraser,* and *pencil.* She puts the object in the bag and asks, "Where's my pencil?" Then, looking into the bag and taking it out, she says, "Here it is!" The teacher repeats the demonstration with other objects.
   Imitation: The teacher asks the students, "Where is your pencil?" The students show their pencils and answer, "Here it is." Repetition with other objects occurs, including body parts.
3. Practice
   Let's chant: Students listen to the audiotape and clap hands to the rhythm. Students chant in two groups, that is, Group A asks, "Where is your nose?" Group B points and answers, "Here it is." The groups exchange roles; volunteer pairs come to the front and perform the dialog; and the teacher verbally rewards the best pairs.

Let's check: The students open the activity book and listen to the sentences and circle the relevant pictures.

4. Assessment

   Students do exercises in the activity book. For example, students find the hidden body parts in the picture and work in groups, saying, "This is . . ." and "Look at the . . ." to show the body parts found: foot, head, face, nose, mouth, ear, eye, arm, finger, leg, body, hand.

   The teacher encourages peer assessment in groups.

5. Additional activities

   Listen to the text recording and read text.

   Read and act.

Improving English Instruction in China

In the United States, the National Reading Panel (NRP) reviewed more than 100,000 studies in reading instruction, focusing on the years of kindergarten through grade 3. The panel identified instructional methods that consistently are related to reading success, and thus an extensive knowledge base now exists to show educators the skills children must learn in order to read well (Center for the Improvement of Early Reading Achievement 2001).

The report identified five areas of reading instruction: phonemic awareness, phonics, fluency, vocabulary, and text comprehension. These same areas can be addressed in China for improving English instruction.

Phonemic Awareness. Phonemic awareness is the ability to notice, think about, and work with the individual sounds in spoken words. Before children learn to read, they need to become aware of how the sounds in words work. They must understand that words are composed of speech sounds, or phonemes. Phonemic awareness includes recognizing which words in a set begin with the same sound, isolating and saying the first or last sound in a word, combining the separate sounds in saying a word, and segmenting a word into its separate sounds.

Adding phonemic awareness instruction to the curriculum would enhance English language learning. Current programs do not include children manipulating phonemes by using letters of the English alphabet nor activities in identifying, blending, segmenting, deleting, or substituting English phonemes. Research conducted by Ashmore, Chu, Farrier, and Paulson (2003) demonstrated that Chinese first- and second-grade students who received explicit instruction in English phonemic awareness outperformed the control group not only in phonemic awareness activities but also in the amount of English words read orally.

Phonics. Phonics is the understanding that there is a predictable relationship between sounds, or phonemes, and graphemes, or the written letters and spellings that represent those sounds. Most Chinese texts include only limited phonics instruction. We recommend providing more opportunities for Chinese children to apply what they are learning about English letters and sounds to the reading of words, sentences, and stories.

Fluency. Fluency is the ability to read a text accurately and quickly. Fluent readers read aloud effortlessly and with expression; fluency bridges word recognition and comprehension. Fluency instruction is currently strong in China. Programs should continue to have students, with guidance, repeatedly read passages aloud and engage in choral reading and tape-assisted reading. Additional instructional approaches, such as partner reading and readers' theater, can be introduced.

Vocabulary. Vocabulary is the words one must know to communicate effectively. It relates to reading comprehension. Readers cannot understand what they are reading without knowing what most of the words mean.

English programs in the PRC involve students engaging in oral language and listening to tapes, but specific word instruction and word learning activities are limited. Additional strategies are recommended, including introducing important vocabulary prior to reading, teaching word parts (prefixes, suffixes, roots), and using context clues to guess the meaning of an unknown word.

Text Comprehension. Text comprehension is understanding what one is reading. Good readers have a purpose for reading; they think actively as they read.

Primary schools in China lack high-quality children's literature written in English. Such books are expensive. However, more children's literature should be used in Chinese classrooms because these stories are an excellent tool for such instructional strategies as using graphic and semantic organizers, generating questions, answering questions, recognizing story structure, and summarizing.

In addition, overall writing instruction should be established. Also, cooperative learning, ad hoc grouping, and flexible grouping should be added to the teacher's repertoire.

Another strategy that Chinese teachers can learn from American language instruction is the use of authentic assessment.

In China, a rigid and comprehensive examination system determines a student's eligibility for advanced training and the form it will take. Beginning in kindergarten, children advance to either key, prestigious elementary schools or to regular primary schools based on their examination scores. In the fifth or sixth year of primary school, test scores determine junior secondary school placements. At the end of the third year of junior secondary school, students take examinations to determine placements in either key senior or regular senior secondary schools, specialized secondary schools, or senior vocational schools. Students who score poorly are placed in junior vocational schools and graduate as "workers."

More authentic assessment activities are recommended to complement the established MOE examination guidelines. In order to use assessments to improve student performance, we recommend the following:

- Classroom observation and the use of anecdotal records and charts so that teachers can track students' language progress.
- Oral miscue analysis, in which the student reads aloud and the teacher notes on the text any repetitions, substitutions, insertions, omissions, or self-corrections the student makes.
- Story retelling, in which the student retells what she has read.

- Story writing, in which the student writes a story in response to a series of pictures or to a wordless picture book.
- Tape recordings of oral reading, in which the student tape-records her oral reading for later review.
- Reading logs, in which the student maintains an ongoing record of the different types of material she is reading.
- Reading-response logs, which are notebooks in which the student records her responses to what she has read, and the teacher replies to the responses.
- Student-teacher conferences in which the student and teacher set goals and discuss the student's progress.

Authentic assessments, coupled with formal tests, help teachers discover more about how their students are approaching, interacting with, and responding to English. The variety of assessment activities shows how the language learner is functioning in phonemic awareness, phonics, fluency, word recognition, and text comprehension. The teacher can then plan and provide the necessary English instruction.

Learning from One Another

Wouldn't it be grand if the United States required all of its third-grade students and older to learn a foreign language? Why not the Chinese language? Foreign language learning promotes multicultural awareness and acceptance; creates an awareness of international economics and defense; encourages leisure activities, especially international travel; and builds bridges between societies (Reagan and Osborn 2002).

The United States and China show many differences in teaching a foreign language. The most readily observable difference is that the United States does not require students to learn a second language. But the U.S. language courses that are offered are much different than foreign language courses in China. Chinese foreign language courses are characterized by whole-group instruction. Recitation and memorization are the dominant teaching methods, and the textbook is the primary resource for the class. U.S. classes use a variety of student groupings for instruction. U.S. teachers also use a wide variety of teaching techniques, and the textbooks are supplemented with many different materials.

China now is a member of the World Trade Organization and is positioned to benefit from the achievements of peoples and countries far from its shores. China also is positioned to enrich others around the world.

China's goals are to build a modern economy and a sound education system and to strengthen ties with the United States. Neither country will achieve what it wants, and needs, if differences overshadow common goals. It is hoped that the 21st century will be one of peace between our countries, a century in which our nations compete and cooperate educationally, economically, and scientifically to the benefit of both our peoples.

References

Ashmore, R.A., and Cao, Z. *Teacher Education in the People's Republic of China.* Bloomington, Ind.: Phi Delta Kappa Educational Foundation, 1997.

Ashmore, R.A.; Chu, X.; Farrier, M.J.; and Paulson, L.H. "The Effects of Phonemic Awareness Drills on Phonological Awareness and Word Reading Performance in a Later Learned Alphabetic Script." *Reading Improvement* 40, no. 1 (2003): 33-47.

Braunger, Jane, and Lewis, Jan Patricia. *Building a Knowledge Base in Reading*. Urbana, Ill.: National Council of Teachers of English, 1997.

Cambridge Young Learners English (CYLE). "What's Cambridge Young Learners English?" 2001. http://www.xinzhitang.com.cn/intro/index_e.htm

Center for the Improvement of Early Reading Achievement. *Put Reading First: The Research Building Blocks for Teaching Children to Read*. Washington, D.C.: Partnership for Reading, 2001.

Department of Planning and Construction. *Educational Statistics Yearbook of China, 1999.* Beijing: People's Education Press, 1999.

Ellis, Printha, ed. *New Standard English*. Beijing: Foreign Language Teaching and Research Press, Macmillan, 2000.

Foreign Language Teaching and Research Press (FLTRP). "Primary and Middle School English." 2002. http://www.fltrp.com/en/english14.html

Graddol, D. *The Future of English*. Manchester, Eng.: British Council, 1997. http://www.lingomedia.com/products/markets.html

Lingo Media. "Markets." 30 October 2002. http://www.lingomedia.com/products/markets.html

Liu, D. *Analecta on English in Schools*. Beijing: Beijing Normal University Press, 2001.

Ministry of Education. *A Guidance for Energetic Implementation of English in Primary Schools*. Beijing, 2001. a

Ministry of Education. *Basic Requirements for Primary English Teaching (Experimental Version)*. Beijing, 2001. b

Ministry of Education. *Outline of Curriculum Reform in Basic Education (Experimental Version)*. Beijing, 2001. c

"Olympic Bidding Success Spurs English Language Fever in China." *People's Daily Online*, 29 July 2001.

PEP English Teacher's Manual Book 1. Beijing: People's Education Press, Lingo Media, 2001.

PEP Primary English. Beijing: People's Education Press, Lingo Media, 2001.

Qiu, Y.; Wang, J.; and Liang, Q. *Cambridge Young Learners English*. Xi'an, Shanxi Province, China: Xi'an Jiao Tong University Press, 2000.

Reagan, T.G., and Osborn, T.A. *The Foreign Language Educator in Society*. Mahwah, N.J.: Lawrence Erlbaum Associates, 2002.

State Council, PRC. "Reform and Development of Basic Education." Document 2001-21. Beijing, 2001.

Teacher Personnel Department of the MOE. *Research on Foreign Language Training in Basic Education #6*. Beijing: People's Education Press, 2001.

"Zeal to Learn Languages." *China Daily*, 9 October 2002.

Appendix A

A Guidance for Energetic Implementation of English in Primary Schools

Ministry of Education, 2001

I. Energetically implement English courses in primary schools.

Starting fall semester 2001, primary schools in cities and county towns should gradually offer English courses; primary schools in townships would commence English teaching fall semester 2002, generally beginning in grade 3. While introducing English teaching, those schools already teaching other foreign languages, such as Japanese and Russian, should be supported to retain these courses; research focusing on the effects of double-foreign-language should be encouraged.

II. Basic requirements for primary English course.

In alignment with the *Basic Requirements for Primary English Teaching (Experimental version)*, the priorities are to foster the learners' interest in learning English, a sense of speech and solid basis of phonetics, and to encourage students to communicate in simple English. The method that highlights the teaching of phonetic and grammatical knowledge should be avoided and corrected. The core of teaching primary students is to develop students' ability to and interest in communicating in English. Assessing learning in accordance with the course objectives and adopting formative evaluation instruments are recommended.

Following the principle of short lessons with high frequency, schools should integrate long and short periods and in-class and after-class learning involving enriched instructional activities. At least four instruction occurrences should be guaranteed per week. In order to do so, one period of Chinese language arts and other electives will be eliminated to give way to English teaching.

According to the conditions available, teachers should use reformed teaching models. Rather than the traditional teaching stereotype, utilization of technology and audio and video teaching resources to provide supportive language learning settings are encouraged. In areas lacking qualified teachers, instructional activities will be supplemented with active employment of resources, (television, videotapes, CD-ROMs, and audiotapes).

Starting in early 2001, China Education Television (CETV) will broadcast training programs for primary English teachers to promote their teaching capability, and from September 2001 some primary English teaching programs will be provided, accompanied with audio and video resources.

III. Tightening textbook management.

All the present primary English course books should be examined according to the guidelines in *Basic Re-*

quirements for Primary English Teaching (Experimental version). Only those approved would be listed in the Textbook Catalogue; those unlisted will be removed. The MOE must approve new textbooks. The development of high-quality English teaching software / courseware should be supported.

IV. Intensifying the training of the primary English teachers.

Training primary English teachers is essential to the improvement of English teaching quality. To meet the demand for teaching the new English courses, initially, the emphasis should be on training lead teachers and assistant teachers. Train current inservice teachers who have some English foundation and shift their assignments to those of teaching English. Junior normal colleges, teacher-training schools, and teaching and research departments should play an active role in inservice teacher training under the guidance of local education administrations.

In order to raise the capacity and capability of training elementary school English teachers, normal colleges should develop English education programs. They should continue to offer secondary foreign languages, as well, and encourage normal schools to offer specialized English programs. Secondary normal schools should require English as part of the curriculum; normal schools with sufficient resources should be restructured to secondary foreign language normal schools. Local administration should devise favorable policies to attract good English teachers and encourage non-normal college English major graduates to teach English in primary schools.

V. Strengthening the leadership of primary English courses.

Education administrations at various levels must realize the importance of mandating English courses in primary schools and strengthen the leadership, planning, and progress steadily. Necessary equipment and resources should be allocated.

To reinforce the primary English curriculum and instruction, the MOE proposes to establish the National Guide Committee for Primary School English Teaching. Teaching and research departments at various levels would assign a specialized researcher to supervise and promote English-teaching research.

Finally, model classes, model schools, and model districts specializing in English teaching should be established. Central to their mission would be educational research in English teaching and instruction and its dissemination.

Appendix B

Outline of Curriculum Reform in Basic Education (Experimental version)

Ministry of Education, 2001

Education's goals are to promote patriotism, collectivism, and the love of socialism; to perpetuate Chinese and revolutionary tradition; and to promote socialist, democratic, and legal awareness, obedient to state law and societal morality. The new generation shall embrace:

- positive values in life;
- a sense of social responsibility and service to the people with sensitivity to scientific and humane accomplishment and awareness of environment;
- the basic knowledge, skills, and methods for lifelong learning;
- physical and psychological well-being characterized by healthy, aesthetic sentiment coupled with ideals, morality, literacy, and discipline.

In order to achieve quality education, the MOE advocates curriculum reform in basic education. This includes designing systematic nine-year compulsory curriculum. In primary schools, integrated curriculum is the mainstream. In the lower primary grades, the curriculum is moral character and life, language arts, math, physical education, music, and fine arts. The upper primary grades curriculum is ideology and morality, language arts, mathematics, foreign language, comprehensive practice, physical education, music, and fine arts. In the junior high grades, a combination of subjects and integrated curriculum is offered, including ideology and morality, language arts, mathematics, foreign language, science (physics, chemistry, biology), history and society (or history and geography), physical education and health, art (music and fine arts), and comprehensive societal practice. Integrated courses are advocated, and schools are encouraged to offer elective courses. In the compulsory education period, handwriting should be emphasized in language arts, art, and fine arts courses.

Appendix C

Basic Requirements for Primary English Teaching (Experimental version)

Ministry of Education, 2001

Globalization has made foreign languages, especially English, an important tool in China's reform and opening-up with the international community. Recently, English has been offered at more primary schools and in more areas, and research findings have supported its benefits. In order to fully implement quality education and to enhance the quality of the whole nation in the 21st century, the MOE has actively mandated English in primary schools. *Basic Requirements for Primary English Teaching (Experimental version)* is the basis for implementation and evaluation of primary English instruction and for the examination and selection of course books.

I. Goals of the course

With recognition to age and psychological characteristics, the goals for primary English courses are to stimulate children's interest in and positive attitude toward learning English, to develop confidence and sense of speech, and to lay the foundation of phonetics for further English study.

II. Starting grade and schedule

Primary English is offered from grade 3. In order to guarantee quality of instruction, the teaching program must combine regular and shorter lesson spans with high frequency. A minimum of four classes per week is required with shorter durations for grades 3 and 4; a combination of regular and shorter lessons is required for grades 5 and 6, including at least two regular lessons per week.

III. Instructional goals and standards

There are two levels of standards for primary English curriculum. Level 1 applies to grades 3 and 4; level 2 applies to grades 5 and 6. As the conditions for English education vary in different areas, with the approval of the provincial education administration, a modified level 2 standard (higher or lower) may be implemented.

Level 1 student outcomes are as follows:

Listening and doing

1. Identify pictures or objects according to the words heard.
2. Respond correctly to classroom instructions.
3. Act according to the instructions, for example, point to pictures, color, draw, or act.
4. Understand simple stories with visual prompts and respond.

Speaking and singing
1. Listen to a recording and imitate.
2. Greet each other.
3. Exchange simple personal information, such as names and ages.
4. Express simple feelings, such as likes and dislikes.
5. Guess and speak mimed actions.
6. Sing 15-20 simple English songs and 15-20 chants.
7. Say words or short sentences about accompanying pictures.

Playing and performing
1. Play games in English and communicate in English while playing.
2. Role play.
3. Perform English songs and fairy tales.

Reading and writing
1. Using visual aids, write the word.
2. Read aloud the learned words.
3. Read and comprehend simple stories with pictures.
4. Correctly print words and sentences.

Viewing and listening
1. Understand simple English cartoons and teaching programs (minimal audiovisual practice time is 10 hours per school year or 20-25 minutes per week).

Level 2 student outcomes are:

Listening
1. Understand slow but natural speech or audiotape with the prompt of pictures and gestures.

2. Understand simple stories with illustrations.
3. Understand simple questions in class activities.
4. Understand common directions and requests and respond appropriately.

Speaking

1. Speak English with clear pronunciation, correct stress, and expressive intonation.
2. Make simple dialogues about a familiar person and family.
3. Properly use the basic daily pattern, such as greetings, farewell, gratitude, and apologies.
4. Tell short stories with teacher's prompt.

Reading

1. Pronounce the learned words.
2. Spell simple words according to the spelling rules.
3. Understand the simple directions and requests in the textbooks.
4. Understand the simple message on greeting cards.
5. Understand simple stories and passages with pictures and read in groups.
6. Read aloud the learned texts or stories correctly (total vocabulary for primary school is 600-700 English words).

Writing

1. Write simple titles or descriptions for pictures or objects.
2. Write sentences after the models.
3. Write simple greetings.
4. Punctuate correctly.

Playing and performing

1. Play games in English.
2. Act out short stories or fairy tales with the teacher's help.
3. Perform 30-40 chants and rhymes (including those in level 1).
4. Sing 30-40 English songs.

Viewing and listening

1. Understand simple English cartoons and teaching programs that parallel the learned text (minimal audiovisual practice time is 10 hours per school year or 20-25 minutes per week).

IV. Teaching models and methods

An activity-based instructional model of teaching English should be devised in accordance with young learners' cognitive and affective developmental stages. Priority should be given to language communicative ability. No grammar concepts should be explained; instead, teaching should involve full use of the teaching resources and activities of listening, acting, speaking, playing, and performing in English.

In terms of teaching students in grades 5 and 6, teachers should reinforce their listening and speaking and develop their reading and writing ability.

V. Course books and resources

Primary school English textbooks should complement children's cognitive abilities, develop their interest and sense of speech, and enhance their knowledge and attitudes of the culture and customs in English-speaking countries. Textbooks should promote communicative abilities and global understandings. Teaching should incorporate modern, multimedia instructional technology, such as audiotapes, videos, broadcasting, and television, to support language learning settings and practice opportunities.

VI. Instructional assessment

Various and optional ways of assessing students' English learning should be used. Formative assessment is advocated based on the learner's interest, attitude, and communicative ability in all English learning activities. In most cases, the semester or academic year assessment for students in grades 3 and 4 involve no written tests; rather, a student's performance in the language activities is the basis for assessment. For students in grades 5 and 6, both oral and written tests may be offered, with the oral test focused on the candidate's language ability in real-life situations and the written test focused on listening and reading skills.

Summative assessment shall be recorded in graded or pass-fail format. The use of rankings for appraising or selection is not recommended.

Order Form

SHIP TO:		
STREET		
CITY/STATE OR PROVINCE/ZIP OR POSTAL CODE		
DAYTIME PHONE NUMBER		PDK MEMBER ID NUMBER

QUANTITY	*TITLE*	*PRICE*
	SUBTOTAL	
	Indiana residents add 6% Sales Tax	
	PROCESSING CHARGE	
	TOTAL	

ORDERS MUST INCLUDE PROCESSING CHARGE

Total Merchandise	*Processing Charge*
Up to $50	$5
$50.01 to $100	$10
More than $100	$10 plus 5% of total

Special shipping available upon request.
Prices subject to change without notice.

☐ Payment Enclosed (check payable to Phi Delta Kappa International)

Bill my ☐ VISA ☐ MasterCard ☐ American Express ☐ Discover

ACCT # DATE

EXP DATE SIGNATURE

Mail or fax your order to: Phi Delta Kappa International, P.O. Box 789, Bloomington, IN 47402-0789. USA
Fax: (812) 339-5556. Phone: (812) 339-1156

For fastest service, phone 1-800-766-1156 and use your credit card.